30 Minutes
... To Deal With
Difficult People

Valerie Sutherland
and
Cary Cooper

**KOGAN
PAGE**

First published in 1997
Reprinted 1998, 2000

Kogan Page Limited
120 Pentonville Road
London N1 9JN

British Library Cataloguing in Publication Data

A CIP record for this book is available from the British Library.

ISBN 0 7494 2524 5

Typeset by Saxon Graphics Ltd, Derby
Printed and bound in Great Britain by Clays Ltd, St Ives plc.

CONTENTS

The 30 Minutes Series

The *Kogan Page 30 Minutes Series* has been devised to give your confidence a boost when faced with tackling a new skill or challenge for the first time.

So the next time you're thrown in at the deep end and want to bring your skills up to scratch or pep up your career prospects, turn to the *30 Minutes Series* for help!

Titles available are:

30 Minutes Before Your Job Interview
30 Minutes Before a Meeting
30 Minutes Before a Presentation
30 Minutes to Boost Your Communication Skills
30 Minutes to Brainstorm Great Ideas
30 Minutes to Deal with Difficult People
30 Minutes to Succeed in Business Writing
30 Minutes to Master the Internet
30 Minutes to Make the Right Decision
30 Minutes to Make the Right Impression
30 Minutes to Plan a Project
30 Minutes to Prepare a Job Application
30 Minutes to Write a Business Plan
30 Minutes to Write a Marketing Plan
30 Minutes to Write a Report
30 Minutes to Write Sales Letters

Available from all good booksellers.
For further information on the series, please contact:

Kogan Page, 120 Pentonville Road, London N1 9JN
Tel: 0171 278 0433 Fax: 0171 837 6348

1

DEALING WITH DIFFICULT PEOPLE IN THE WORKPLACE: SCOPE, AIMS AND STRATEGIES

People! Can't live with them ... can't live without them!

The quality of human relationships plays a vital role in determining our health and well-being and the workplace can offer opportunities to develop the social support networks that appear to protect us against the strains and pressures of modern-day living. It is suggested that work colleagues represent a type of substitute family group, and rare are those individuals who can successfully work and thrive in social isolation. While it might be said that it is unlikely we will thrive without the presence of other people around us, there are some people in the workplace whom we might prefer to live without. It seems that we cannot live without them, but we also find it very difficult to live and work with them!

Certain people inhabit our work space to make our lives difficult, unpleasant and unhappy and, as JP Sartre remarked, 'Hell is other people ... and learning to live with other people is one of the most stressful aspects of life.' Some of us have colleagues who frustrate and irritate us to the point of anger; they let us down; criticize what we do; try to boss us around; dominate meetings or discussions; never say what they mean or talk about us behind our backs; or they bore us to death with their constant complaining and whining! Many people suffer a 'difficult boss' who drives us in our work to meet difficult time deadlines and unrealistic goals; never asks for our view or opinion; fails to back or support our decisions or actions when we need it; is inconsiderate; aggressive; and a bully. In addition, people can also find that they are working at what is known as, the 'boundary' of the organization, and are required to deal with difficult and unreasonable customers or clients as part of the job. Since the customer is usually right, and will complain when we fail to handle their awkward or rude behaviour towards us, we run a risk of losing the job if we lose the customer!

Indeed, the behaviour of these 'difficult people' towards us can have negative consequences for us in terms of ineffective performance, poor productivity, ill-health and poor psychological well-being, when our personal resources are already stretched to the limit in trying to cope with the demands of the job and the work environment. How to deal more effectively with 'difficult' people is the topic of this book.

The aims of this book

Our aims are to increase your awareness about the behaviours and actions of 'difficult' people in the workplace and to consider the most effective strategies in eliminating or minimizing the negative impact of their behaviour on your own performance, well-being and the quality of work life.

Who are 'difficult people'?

It should be noted that we all have the potential to be 'difficult people'. As individuals we are unique and possess various distinctive personality traits and behavioural characteristics which can be the source of stimulation, fun and joy for some people, but a cause of irritation, anger and annoyance for others. Thus, we all have the potential to be 'difficult' towards the people around us at work, and according to Ralph Waldo Emerson, the American philosopher and poet, 'we all boil at different degrees'.

Therefore, self-awareness about our own style of behaviour and an understanding about the motivations underlying difficult behaviour are the first steps to improving interpersonal relationships in the workplace, without resorting to actions which exacerbate the situation. Indeed, it is some cause for concern that the incidence of violence at work and reported bullying is on the increase, and this may, in part, be due to our inappropriate ways of managing the behaviours of the difficult people around us, in the high-pressure work environment of contemporary organizational life.

Recognizing our infamous trio of difficult people!

While we *all* have the potential to be 'difficult', there are three well-known stereotypes in the workplace who will be the focus of this book. They might be your boss, a colleague, or someone who works for you. While some are more difficult to deal with because of the nature of the relationship, the outcome will often to be the same since they make life difficult, with costly consequences for you and the business community. Our difficult people include:

- the abrasive personality
- the Type A stress-prone personality
- the aggressive personality

Dealing with difficult people – the strategy of this book

Each of the following chapters on 'difficult' people at work will adopt the same format.

1. In the first section we help you to identify and recognize the 'difficult' individual in the workplace. A brief questionnaire is provided for you to either rate your own behaviour or to measure your perceptions about your boss or other work colleagues.
2. The next section aims to improve your understanding of the reasons why these individuals are difficult and what motivates their behaviour. This sets the scene for Chapter 5 which offers strategies for dealing with difficult people in the workplace

In Chapter 5 we provide a variety of approaches for dealing with such people. We acknowledge that there is no clear-cut stereotypical behaviour, so it is not possible to provide a simple, prescriptive way of dealing with a difficult person. Since there is not just one problem, neither is there just one solution! The choice of strategy will depend both on the circumstance in which you find yourself and the degree to which you feel comfortable handling the situation, and so it is likely to be more effective if you have a repertoire of coping options at your disposal. However, when possible, recommendations for action in dealing with certain, specific 'difficult' behaviours have been outlined in the second part of this chapter.

Finally, Chapter 6, offers guidelines for action planning. This acknowledges that it is rarely possible to change any situation overnight and so you will need to set objectives, define a strategy and set out a plan.

However, first we need to begin with some basic assumptions about difficult people at work.

Why are people difficult?

Before we examine each of these workplace characters in detail it is necessary to understand some basic principles about behaviour and the motivation for 'difficult' behaviour, since this information will be important in guiding the ways in which we attempt to cope with such events. Five simple premises should be remembered:

1: *Behaviour is determined by its consequences*

So, if something nice happens as a result of our behaviour it is likely that we will continue to behave in the way that immediately preceded the outcome. Likewise, if something nasty is taken away as a result of our behaviour we also continue to behave in the way we did immediately prior to the outcome. Indeed, the reverse also applies because we will cease behaviour if something nasty occurs as a results of our actions, or something nice is taken away. This is commonly referred to as 'punishment'. These are known as the 'reinforcers' of behaviour.

This just seems 'common sense psychology' and it simply means that people learn to behave in certain ways because they gain some form of reward and/or avoid behaving in ways that result in punishment or failure to gain a reward. So, this leads to:

2: Behaviour that is rewarded will continue

So, if you are continually having similar problems, it is likely that some aspect of your own behaviour is encouraging this. Recognizing this by careful self-analysis and changing your *own* behaviour can be a significant step forward in handling difficult people in the workplace. This brings us now to premise 3.

3: Behaviour that is punished or not rewarded will cease

This simple statement would appear to lead us to the notion, therefore, that to stop undesirable behaviour, we only have to administer punishment or ensure that the individual does not gain any benefit from their difficult behaviour. While the use of non-reward might be an effective way of changing another person's unwanted behaviour, the use of punishment, even if it were possible, is not likely to change behaviour, because we cannot fulfil the conditions that must exist if it is to be an effective way of changing unwanted behaviour. That is:

4: Punishment is only effective in changing behaviour when the behaviour is punished immediately after it occurs AND the behaviour is punished every time it occurs

From this we can now see that there are only two strategies which are appropriate when seeking to change behaviour, but both of these also require us to change our own behaviour by:

Using positive reinforcement in order to encourage the desired behaviour to occur more often.

1. In a very specific way, identify the observable behaviour to be increased.
2. Identify the reinforcer (also known as the reward) you intend to use. Not all people respond in the same way to reinforcers and so the main difficulty is finding out what

is effective for that particular individual. Smiles and praise are very powerful social reinforcers; special attention, privileges or increased opportunities to participate and take responsibility might also be effective:

3. To be successful reinforcement should immediately follow the display of the desired behaviour.

4. Initially it is appropriate to reinforce every display of the desired behaviour.

5. When the new pattern is established it is possible to maintain the behaviour by changing to what is described as a 'variable ratio reinforcement schedule'. More simply put, it means that it is more effective to only reward a behaviour at variable times, rather than every time, because the individual knows that they will receive a reward (or pay-off) at sometime, and so they keep trying.

Using non-reward means that you need to find a way of ensuring that the 'difficult' work colleague does not gain any benefit from their behaviour towards you. Non-reward leads to the extinction of undesirable behaviours. It is not the same as ignoring the behaviour, rather that the work colleague does not get any positive reward as a consequence. It means that you will need to change the way in which you relate to the other person. So, premise 5 states:

5. *It is important to acknowledge that to change the behaviour of another person, you first must change your own behaviour!*

2

THE ABRASIVE PERSONALITY

This 'difficult person' was originally identified and described in 1978 by Harry Levinson from the Harvard University Medical School. Before you read on, use the questionnaire below to assess the characteristics typically associated with abrasive behaviour in the workplace and identify either: your tendency to be abrasive with other people, or to rate your perceptions of a 'difficult' boss or colleague in the workplace.

Rate each item on the scale below by circling the number which best describes your own behaviour or your perceptions of another person's behaviour at work.

Circle '1' if the statement definitely *does not* sound like a description of your (or your boss or a colleague's) manner of behaviour towards other people; or '7' if it definitely *does* describe the usual style of behaviour.

Item	DISAGREE No, definitely not: score 1			AGREE Yes, definitely: score 7			
1. You regard yourself as more competent than the people around you	1	2	3	4	5	6	7
2. People are clear that you feel more competent than them by your behaviour towards them	1	2	3	4	5	6	7
3. You are condescendingly critical of other people's efforts	1	2	3	4	5	6	7
4. Your comments take up a disproportionate amount of time in discussions and meetings	1	2	3	4	5	6	7
5. You need to feel in control	1	2	3	4	5	6	7
6. You are quick to challenge and rise to the attack	1	2	3	4	5	6	7
7. In conversation you use the word 'I' excessively	1	2	3	4	5	6	7
8. You prefer to remain distant and emotionally cold with the people around you	1	2	3	4	5	6	7
9. Debates and discussions that you are involved in quickly become arguments	1	2	3	4	5	6	7
10. Other people's suggestions and ideas tend to be either inane or mostly useless	1	2	3	4	5	6	7
11. You drive yourself hard	1	2	3	4	5	6	7
12. You tend to regard other people in the workplace as rivals	1	2	3	4	5	6	7
13. You find it difficult to compromise once you have made up your mind	1	2	3	4	5	6	7
14. You tend to view the people around you as 'generally incompetent'	1	2	3	4	5	6	7
15. In meetings and discussions, in your presence, other people tend not to speak up and contribute ideas or suggestions	1	2	3	4	5	6	7
16. You are a perfectionist	1	2	3	4	5	6	7
17. Symbols of status and power are very important to you	1	2	3	4	5	6	7

(adapted from Levinson, 1978)

Score = _____ Plot your total score below

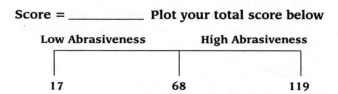

The higher the score received on this questionnaire, the more firmly an individual can be classified as an abrasive personality. For example, 119 points is the highest score possible and indicates the maximum in abrasiveness as a style of behaviour towards other people. It is important to understand that there are no distinct divisions between abrasiveness and non-abrasiveness, because people fall somewhere on a continuum leaning more towards one style of behaviour than another. Sixty-eight is an average score; that is, it is the mid-point and anyone above that is inclined towards an abrasive personality. It suggests that your interpersonal style might be regarded by your work colleagues as 'difficult'.

Characteristics of the abrasive personality

The precise identification of a 'difficult' behavioural tendency is the first step in dealing with a problem and is crucial in the effective implementation of change. It allows you: to remain focused on a specific problem and avoids bringing emotional issues into an already heated situation;

Therefore, if you remember to only concern yourself with the specific behaviour which you find difficult to cope with, or which adversely impacts your own behaviour or performance at work, the chances of bringing about a change in that behaviour are more likely.

While clear-cut stereotypes are rare, it is suggested that an abrasive person is characterized by many of the following traits and ways of behaving:

- stubbornness
- tactlessness; a sharp tongue; blunt
- dismissive of your ideas; highly critical of your efforts
- condescending towards you
- everything you do must be cleared by him/her
- never willing to offer a compromise; perfectionists
- dominate the discussion in meetings
- constantly make you feel incompetent
- impatient with what they regard as irrelevant detail
- only their own demanding standards are acceptable
- drive themselves hard; must be in control
- confrontational and likely to attack when challenged
- distant and emotionally cold towards you
- treat you as a rival
- debate and discussions usually develop into an argument
- preoccupied with symbols of power and status.

When you have decided which of the above behaviours exhibited by a work colleague is causing you distress, you can begin to define your strategy and action plan for dealing with this undesirable situation at work.

Why are people abrasive?

For most of us, it is hard to understand what motivates one person to be unpleasant towards another work colleague. It is even more strange that we must try to comprehend, that often, the abrasive work colleague does want to be liked by other people, by engaging in a job or task that is performed so perfectly that it wins approval and admiration. This, indeed, seems to be part of their problem

17

because they are highly driven by these needs, their judgement becomes impaired and a negative situation develops.

We have already established that for a behaviour to continue, it must in some way be rewarding to the individual. Thus a 'difficult' behaviour is sustained because the individual is gaining more in the form of a reward than in punishment by their actions. It is also suggested that the abrasive personality is an intellectual bully. They are often intelligent and quick-thinking and work their way to the top because of this style of behaviour, and *this* is their reward. The *system* or organization is rewarding them with recognition and promotion and their uncompromising standards, stubbornness and tactlessness arise from the need to be perfect so they can continue on this path to career success. It explains why they must keep control of the situation and usually end up doing the job themselves, because no one else can meet their exacting standards. Such tendencies can result in faulty judgement, leading to impatience with colleagues and a dismissive and rather condescending style of behaviour. Towards the boss they may be fawning, but everyone else is likely to be dominated and viewed as a potential rival. Working in a team is abhorrent to the abrasive personality!

Consequences of the abrasive personality in the workplace

Clearly, work colleagues regard this person as 'difficult' and this leads to poor interpersonal relationships at work, low levels of moral and self-esteem. Poor interactions within the team will be evident and job satisfaction levels are likely to be low.

Perhaps, however, it is subordinates who are most likely to feel the strain of exposure to a difficult, abrasive boss.

In the extreme he/she will rule staff with an iron hand, and is unlikely to show satisfaction with their efforts, whatever they do. Staff can become totally dependent on this type of boss who must always be told what is going on and personally clear all decisions before action can be taken. Therefore, personnel working for an abrasive boss will prefer to wait to be told what to do rather than incur certain wrath by doing something in the 'wrong' way.

In this work climate, levels of morale are likely to be low. Staff tend to feel helpless because they think that the abrasive boss is 'getting away with it' and even being rewarded with further promotion. This is because the organization usually do not want to lose such a bright, highly motivated employee, who achieves results, often in difficult circumstances. However, in the long-term, the organization suffers the consequences of the behaviour of the abrasive personality.

In addition to the problems already noted, it is likely that the quality of decision-making deteriorates because individuals fail to speak up in front of the abrasive individual because they fear being made to look foolish, or are treated in a condescending, critical manner. Thus, staff will feel controlled, and denied the opportunity to contribute to the decisions that affect them. In such a work environment levels of creativity become stifled.

3

THE TYPE A STRESS-PRONE PERSONALITY

In the late 1950s, cardiologists, Meyer Friedman and Ray Rosenman, described a certain pattern of behaviour among heart attack survivors, which they called the Type A style of behaviour. After many years of research it is now acknowledged that the Type A stress prone style of behaviour, referred to as 'TAB' is a risk factor for heart disease, independent of heredity factors (such as high blood pressure and levels of cholesterol), cigarette smoking, alcohol consumption and obesity. Recent research suggests that it is the hostility component of TAB which is likely to be the factor which increases the risk of a heart attack.

Nevertheless, in addition to being a danger to their own health, the Type A individual is also likely to be a 'difficult person' to handle within the work environment by virtue of their behavioural characteristics. Before you read on, use the simple questionnaire below to rate your own TAB, or to assess your perceptions of a boss or colleague at work. This is based on the work of R.W. Bortner and aims to provide you with a rough guide to the TAB temperament. An absence of Type A behaviour characteristics is called 'Type B' behaviour.

Recognizing the Type A stress-prone person

Circle one number for each of the bi-polar statements below which best reflects the way you behave in your everyday life. For example, if you are generally on time for appointments (the first statement), you would circle a number between 7 and 11. If you are casual about appointments you would circle one of the lower numbers between 1 and 5

Casual about appointments	1 2 3 4 5 6 7 8 9 10 11	Never late
Not competitive	1 2 3 4 5 6 7 8 9 10 11	Very competitive
Good listener	1 2 3 4 5 6 7 8 9 10 11	Anticipates what others are going to say (nods, attempts to finish for them)
Never feels rushed – even when under pressure	1 2 3 4 5 6 7 8 9 10 11	Always rushed
Can wait patiently	1 2 3 4 5 6 7 8 9 10 11	Impatient while waiting
Takes things one at a time	1 2 3 4 5 6 7 8 9 10 11	Tries to do many things at once, thinks about what will do next
Slow, deliberate talker	1 2 3 4 5 6 7 8 9 10 11	Emphatic in speech – fast and forceful
Cares about satisfying him/herself no matter what others may think	1 2 3 4 5 6 7 8 9 10 11	Wants a good job recognized by others
Slow doing things	1 2 3 4 5 6 7 8 9 10 11	Fast – eating walking, etc
Easy-going	1 2 3 4 5 6 7 8 9 10 11	Hard-driving – pushing yourself and others
Expresses feelings	1 2 3 4 5 6 7 8 9 10 11	Hides feelings

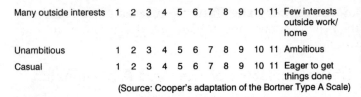

Many outside interests	1	2	3	4	5	6	7	8	9	10	11	Few interests outside work/home
Unambitious		1	2	3	4	5	6	7	8	9	10	11	Ambitious
Casual		1	2	3	4	5	6	7	8	9	10	11	Eager to get things done

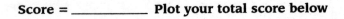

(Source: Cooper's adaptation of the Bortner Type A Scale)

Score = _____ Plot your total score below

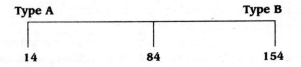

The higher the score received on this questionnaire, the more firmly an individual can be classified as Type A. It is important to understand that there are no distinct divisions between Type A and Type B. Rather, people fall somewhere on a continuum leaning more towards one type of behaviour than another

You should be aware that Type As often deny both the physical and psychological response to strain and are often blind to the extent of their own behaviour. If you are scoring this questionnaire to assess your own personality and suspect that you have tendencies towards a Type A style of behaviour, it is likely that you will find it difficult to be completely honest in answering this form of self-assessment, not because of deliberate intent to be dishonest, but because you simply choose not to be truly aware of the ways in which you prefer to behave. Therefore, in order to get a more accurate assessment, it might be more useful if you also ask someone else who knows you well to complete this questionnaire based on their perceptions about your usual behaviour in the workplace.

Characteristics of the Type A personality

As you look at the list below, consider how the behaviour of the Type A individual can cause them to be labelled, 'difficult'. Are you guilty of being a 'difficult' person?

- Devotion to work; working long hours; feeling guilty when they are not working or are relaxing; tend to take work home evenings and weekends.
- A chronic sense of time urgency – always rushed and working under impossible deadline conditions, with the constant need to hurry also reflected in their overt behaviour since they are likely to move, walk and drive fast, and even eat rapidly. Indeed, Type A behaviour is known as 'the hurry disease'.
- Emphatic gestures such as banging the fist on a table or fist clenching and waving are typical Type A outbursts.
- Attempting to schedule more and more in less and less time. Making few allowances for unforeseen events which might disrupt the work schedule.
- Often attempting to do two or more things at the same time. This is known as 'polyphasic activity'. For example, it is the typical Type A individual who will want to read while eating, or continue to work on a document while talking on the telephone about a completely unrelated event.
- Hates being kept waiting, particularly in queues. This even extends to impatience with the rate at which most events take place. For example, they will prefer to rush up stairs, three-at-a-time, rather than waiting for the lift to arrive. They also have the habit of finishing sentences for other people, or frequently urging

them to the point by interspersing the dialogue with, 'yes, yes, yes', or repeating, 'uh huh' over and over again. Frequent sighing during questioning is a typical Type A trait.

- The actual speech pattern of the Type A individual reflects underlying aggression or hostility by their habit of explosively accentuating various key words into ordinary speech without any real need. They have a strong voice, clipped, rapid and emphatic speech, and the last few words of sentences are rushed out as if to quicken the delivery of what they want to say, thereby exhibiting impatience even with themselves!

- Finds it difficult to talk about anything other than work-related interests and perhaps does not have any interests outside work to discuss with others! Type As do not take all their holiday or are likely to cut a holiday short. They really believe that the workplace cannot function without them!

- Rarely notices things (or people) around them in the workplace that are not related to their job or to the means of getting the job done.

- Highly competitive with themselves and everyone around them. Type A individuals continually set themselves (and other people) goals which they try to beat or better. Since Type A individuals constantly drive themselves (and others) to meet high, often unrealistic standards, it is not surprising that they feel angry when they make a mistake, and experience frustration and easy irritation in the work situation, when they experience failure in achievement or become dissatisfied with the efforts of their work colleagues and subordinates.

- Exhibits a strong need to be in control of events around

them. A perceived lack of control over events will cause Type A individuals to become even more extreme in their time-urgent and hasty behaviours.

Why are people Type A?

The manifestation of Type A behaviour would seem to be a response to a challenge in the environment. By engaging in active coping in threatening situations, the Type A individual remains physiologically aroused, and this constant recurring sympathetic activity is associated with the process of atherosclerosis. While some researchers have tried to claim a heritability component to the Type A behaviour style, it is more likely that it is learned. Indeed, it must be a way of coping which the Type A individual finds rewarding in some way in order for the behaviour pattern to continue.

While the Type A stress-prone behaviour pattern is likely to be costly to an organization in the long-term, the immediate outcome is one of gain from these workaholic individuals. Thus, Type As are both tolerated and rewarded with promotion and privilege by their actions and so their behaviour pattern is reinforced (that is, rewarded).

The Type A individual has been likened to Sisyphus, King of Corinth, who was condemned to roll a huge marble block up a hill, which as soon as it reached the top always rolled down again. This striving against real or imagined odds, irrespective of the outcome, an inability to enjoy the satisfaction of achievement or relax, was the way in which S.G. Wolf perceived and described the stress-prone Type A person.

Consequences of Type A behaviour in the workplace

While the Type A individual is high sociable, work colleagues tend to regard them as 'difficult' because of their constant need to compete and never be defeated. They tend not to listen or let you finish what you want to say, often because they believe they already have the 'perfect' solution to the problem. Indeed, they think they are always right. As work colleagues they are unlikely to be supportive of each other, tend to be poor team-players, and fail to take any personal interest in the people around them.

The subordinates of a Type A boss are likely to feel the strain of exposure to this difficult individual because of their tendency to demand and maintain a strict control over what is going on. Also, Type A bosses often find it quicker to do a job themselves rather than taking time to show someone else what to do, and so they fail to develop their staff and delegate. This, of course, puts them under even more pressure and so their levels of irritability and hostility continue to rise. Thus, the staff of a Type A boss can often experience the stress of qualitative work-underload because they feel under-utilized, not trusted or valued as employees. Rarely are Type A bosses satisfied with the achievements of their staff, and they constantly expect everyone around them to work to their demanding pace and schedule, including long hours of working and skipping lunch breaks in order to meet imposed, and often unrealistic goals and work deadlines.

Ultimately the organization suffers the consequences of the dysfunctional behaviour of the Type A, workaholic, perfectionist individual. Type A individuals often exhibit a reduced level of both physical and psychological well-being and can be job-dissatisfied. As employees (both colleagues and subordinates) become dissatisfied and unable to cope with the pressures of exposure to this mode and style of working, both health and performance standards might suffer. Use of sick leave is likely to rise because staff will 'vote with their feet' and avoid coming into work so they can get a break from a 'difficult' boss.

4

THE AGGRESSIVE PERSONALITY

The aggressive individual always aims to win ... usually at the expense of other people. For them, 'attack is the best form of defence'. They are, in fact, the workplace bullies!

The questionnaire below contains a series of statements about the characteristics of people in the workplace who are 'difficult' because they behave aggressively towards others. Use it to identify either your own aggressive behaviour tendencies towards other people; or to rate your perceptions about the manner of behaviour for your boss or colleague.

Circle one number for each of the statements below which best reflects the way you behave in your everyday life and/or your perceptions of a boss or work colleague's behaviour towards you at work.

Circle '1' if the statement definitely does not sound like a description of your own, or your boss's or a colleague's manner of behaviour towards other people; or '7' if it definitely does describe the usual style of behaviour.

Item	DISAGREE No, definitely not: score 1					AGREE Yes, definitely: score 7
Often state opinion as fact	1	2	3	4	5	6	7
Tend to quickly jump to conclusions	1	2	3	4	5	6	7
Quick to blame others when things go wrong	1	2	3	4	5	6	7
Very likely to resort to the use of sarcasm	1	2	3	4	5	6	7
Quick to put down or devalue other people's ideas	1	2	3	4	5	6	7
Uses extreme hand gestures, eg fist waving, finger pointing, thumping on furniture etc	1	2	3	4	5	6	7
Constantly give advice on what, and how things ought to be done	1	2	3	4	5	6	7
Like to find flaws in the other person's viewpoint	1	2	3	4	5	6	7
Use 'I' frequently	1	2	3	4	5	6	7
Critical of other people	1	2	3	4	5	6	7
Tell others what to do in a threatening manner	1	2	3	4	5	6	7
Shout when angered	1	2	3	4	5	6	7
Boastful of actions	1	2	3	4	5	6	7
Constantly interrupt to give opinion	1	2	3	4	5	6	7
Discourage any feedback about actions or performance	1	2	3	4	5	6	7
Use a confrontational or threatening style when asking questions or giving instructions	1	2	3	4	5	6	7
Rarely consult with other colleagues on how things should be done	1	2	3	4	5	6	7
Like to get 'own way'	1	2	3	4	5	6	7
Resort to piercing, hard stares when displeased or upset	1	2	3	4	5	6	7
Short-tempered	1	2	3	4	5	6	7

Score = _____ Plot your total score below

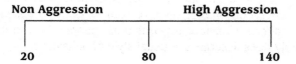

Non Aggression   **High Aggression**

20   80   140

The higher the score received on this questionnaire, the more firmly an individual can be classified as an aggressive personality. For example, 140 points is the highest possible score and indicates the maximum in aggression as a style of behaviour towards other people. It is important to understand that there are no distinct divisions between non-aggression and high-aggression since people fall somewhere on a continuum leaning more towards one style of behaviour than the other. Eighty is an average score; that is, it is the mid-point and anyone above that is inclined towards an aggressive personality. Anyone below the average score is more inclined towards a non-aggressive approach.

Characteristics of the aggressive personality

It is commonly agreed that someone is behaving aggressively towards you when they assert their own rights at the expense of your basic rights (your wants, needs, beliefs, opinions or feelings). Overt displays of aggression show themselves in many different ways and are expressed in varying degrees, taking both verbal and non-verbal forms. The following list offers some guidelines, although it should be remembered that a single, isolated incident of behaviour must be 'read' in context, and alone cannot be taken as 'aggressive'.

Body/Movement

Leans forward arms crossed high over the chest; or hands on hips; unable to sit still/strides about; stands or sits in close proximity to the other people; tense.

Head/Face

Frowns; presses lips tightly together; assumes a set facial expression; in the extreme will bare their teeth; juts the chin out and upwards.

Eyes
Maintains strong eye contact; cold hard stare; piercing/glaring eyes; will be last to look away in the conflict situation.

Hands
Sharp, provocative hand gestures, such as clenched fist, shaking of fist, or finger pointing and stabbing actions.

Voice
Terse, abrupt and threatening speech; cold, loud voice; tends to raise voice at the end of sentences.

Below we describe some examples typical of aggressive behaviour which illustrate why we tend to use the label 'difficult' to describe such individuals in the workplace. They:

- display a lack of interest in your opinions
- will constantly interrupt you with their own opinions
- take you for granted
- are short-tempered and resentful of you
- like to find fault in your work
- are highly critical and sarcastic
- are swift to jump to conclusions
- will always let you know if they feel let down
- tend to be highly vocal and will resort to shouting and swearing
- make decisions that affect you without consultation
- poke fun and try to devalue your ideas
- make their displeasure clearly evident
- are confrontational – issues quickly become a personal attack
- tend to blame others, frequently using 'you' statements
- say exactly what they are thinking, even at the expense of the people around them.

Why are people aggressive?

In simple terms, other people are aggressive towards us because there is an immediate pay-off; that is, they receive a reward, or reinforcement for their behavioural style and so the aggressiveness continues. Being aggressive usually results in the aggressor getting their own way because they assert their rights in a way that ignores the rights of the other person. It is often dishonest and unhelpful, but usually it means that they experience a sense of power over other people. They want to dominate and win. An aggressive style of behaviour is often confused with assertive behaviour, and it has been suggested that 'aggression' is 'assertive' behaviour that has gone wrong, usually when the individual is exposed to a difficult situation. In fact, these people really believe that their approach is simply honest, direct, straight-talking, and people know exactly where they stand.

Interestingly, the root cause of both aggressive and non-assertive behaviours stem from the same core beliefs. In both instances:

- a belief exists that other people or situations are threatening;
- there is a failure to think rationally about one's self;
- there is over-reaction because of previous experiences; that is, displays of earlier non-assertion or aggression have not gone well or as expected; and
- there is a failure to develop the skills of assertion.

Although the immediate reward is satisfying for the aggressive person, it is likely that, in the long-term, they experience feelings of regret, guilt or shame about the ways in which they behaved and treated you. To appease this negative situation they resort to apologizing in a profuse manner; try to make amends by being over helpful; and/or blame someone else for the situation. In this state of affairs their level of self-esteem is damaged and they become angry with themselves. Use of aggression in response to a situation is energy-demanding since the body is required to remain in a high state of physical and psychological alert, and in the long-term, this can cause problems associated with elevated blood pressure.

Consequences of aggressive behaviour in the workplace

From the above it becomes clear why aggressive people are regarded by work colleagues as 'difficult' and how they cause others to feel upset, angry, anxious and lacking in self-worth. Indeed, there is a growing awareness that oppressive behaviour such as this is damaging in terms of well-being, morale, motivation and job performance, and it should not be tolerated or condoned. While in many instances 'the aggrieved' will openly fight back or retaliate, in other circumstances the recipients of aggression suppress their feelings, and harbour desires for revenge. They will find subtle of getting even, for example, by sabotage – failing to fulfil duties or some task that they overtly had to agree to under duress. Clearly, neither open conflict nor stifled hostility are productive workplace behaviours.

An aggressive boss who rules by fear may ultimately suffer as staff try to get even by underhand means. For example, appearing to cooperate but resorting to back-biting and delay in work activities at every chance. They will be quite happy to let an aggressive boss dig his/her own grave, and even help this process by letting a bad decision or mistake made by the boss proceed to some ultimate bitter end. Indeed, this might be the only way staff will be able to retaliate and rid themselves of a tyrant!

Therefore, the organization also suffers from the costs of aggression as performance deteriorates, when people ultimately quit, or are frequently absent from work to avoid an aggressive boss or work colleague. If employees are fearful about 'speaking out' it is possible that poor quality decisions are made since ideas are not fully discussed. If the 'questioning people' actually leave the organization because they are not prepared to tolerate working with aggressive work colleagues, or an aggressive boss, it is likely that the people who stay will be the ones who 'keep their heads below the parapet' and thereby avoid risky conflict behaviour. This means that levels of creativity within the organization are likely to suffer. Those people who would normally temper risky decisions are also repressed and might even be prepared, and quietly pleased, to let an aggressive colleague 'pay' for an error of judgement.

However, it is possible that a powerful, aggressive individual is often admired because they seem to get their own way and get things done. Thereby, they become a role model for junior staff, building and reinforcing an aggressive, power culture within the workplace, which could be harmful to the organization.

5

COPING WITH DIFFICULT PEOPLE IN THE WORKPLACE

A variety of techniques and strategies are available for dealing with difficult people in the workplace. In the next section we will consider certain approaches to help us cope more effectively with our trio of our difficult characters including the

- *abrasive personality*
- *Type A stress-prone personality*
- *aggressive personality*

First, some general approaches, applicable to all these difficult people will be considered, including

- *anger and conflict management*
- *dealing with criticism*
- *role negotiation*

Finally, some specific ways of dealing with each of our difficult people will be put forward.

Precise identification of a 'difficult' person in terms of their actual behaviour towards you is the first step in dealing effectively with the problem and is crucial to the effective management of change. It allows you to:

- remain focused on a specific problem and avoids bringing emotional issues into an already heated situation
- refrain from making generalized comments and attack on the individual's personality or attitude, which would certainly result in argument or denial, since most people are likely to resent criticism or mild comment about their core functioning.

Therefore, it is crucial that you remember to only concern yourself with the specific behaviour with which you are finding coping difficult, and/or which results in an adverse impact on your performance or well-being. This will increase your chances of bringing about an improvement in the situation, and a desired change in behaviour.

Anger and conflict management

Without a doubt, it is likely that exposure to the people described in the chapters above can make us angry. Also, in some instances we must learn how to respond to the anger directed at us. Quite plainly, when we become angry and distressed, we cannot respond by fighting back since this is not socially acceptable in organizational life, but neither can we run away from the situation because we must fulfil our job and role commitments. Losing control by losing your temper might cause you to lose your job or face disciplinary action. It will certainly cause you to lose the respect of the people you work with and earn *you* the label of 'difficult person'.

Indeed, resorting to a 'fight' or 'flight' response is psychologically damaging because it harms our self-esteem when we fail to gain mastery in a situation. However, the alarm reaction, known as 'fight or flight' is the normal physiological response to such stress-provoking situations and denial can cause us to experience frustration and stress-related psychosomatic disorders.

A combination of chemical transmitters known as adrenaline and noradrenaline are involved in the 'fight or flight' response. It is noradrenaline which is mainly responsible for our 'fight' response and makes us feel excited and aroused, and induces fighting behaviours, which include standing straight and tall, with the tiny hairs on the body standing on end (the original aim of this was to make our hairy ancestors look larger than their opponent), showing and grinding of our teeth, making threatening gestures and loud vocal sounds. Adrenaline induces the feelings of fear associated with wanting to run away from an opponent; for example, wanting to leave or 'run away' from the room just before an examination commences!

In response to the long-term demands of exposure to stress, cortisol is mobilized to increase the supply of glucose and fatty acids in the bloodstream. In vigorous activity it will break down lean tissue for conversion to sugar as an additional source energy and will also block the removal of certain acids in the bloodstream. In excess this will cause stomach ulcers because of increased acid formation. Cortisol also inhibits immunity and inflammatory responses.

In physiological terms when the body is prepared for fight or flight, we experience:

■ faster breathing to supply more oxygen needed for the muscles

- pounding heart as the heart speeds up and blood pressure rises as it forces blood around the body
- butterflies in the stomach or indigestion as digestive processes slow so blood may be redirected to the brain and muscles
- quicker thinking as brain activity is stimulated
- release of fats and sugars from storage deposits to provide fuel for energy
- increased sweating to cool the body as it burns more energy
- tense muscles ready for action, resulting in neck– or backache following a stressful situation
- dry mouth as the supply of saliva decreases
- larger pupils as they dilate for keener vision.

Therefore, exposure to a situation which persistently triggers our alarm reaction and induces either a 'fight or flight' response which is denied, is in the long-term potentially harmful to both our physical and psychological well-being. When we lead an increasingly sedentary lifestyle we are denied the physical activity which would be a natural outlet for the build-up of the stress response, and thereby we expose ourselves to increased risks of stress-related illness.

Understanding conflict

It is important to acknowledge that the human condition is fraught with conflict which is unavoidable in our modern-day lifestyle. Both society and business life are filled with potential for conflict situations (for example, political instability and uncertainty; increasing crime rates; likelihood of divorce; the premature death of loved ones due to heart disease and cancer; job reorganization, change, insecurity and redundancies). Therefore, it is more productive to expect that conflict will inevitably exist to disrupt, but it need not destroy.

'Not all conflict is bad' is a belief which is consistent with the view that one cannot make an omelette without breaking eggs! It means that honest, openly expressed conflict, at the appropriate time, can be beneficial for our development and protect us from damage. However, suppression, and the withholding of hostile feelings, or bottling anger up inside, can be damaging to both our self- esteem and our heart (remember, the Type A individual who internalizes hostility and anger is at increased risk from heart disease). Conflict is also beneficial since it can help us to break free of the bounds of convention and is, therefore, essential for creativity and innovation because it provides a spur to challenge, growth, development and change. We should keep in mind that 'functional conflict' works towards the goals of the organization, the group and the individual, but 'dysfunctional conflict' blocks goal achievement, frustrates and irritates.

There is nothing wrong with feeling angry when a work colleague or boss lets you down, does not support you when the situation gets tough, or acts in an inconsiderate way towards you. However, it is how you choose to behave and act on these feelings which is important in the work environment. Repressed anger over extended periods of time may be converted into elevated blood pressure, and so anger must be actively managed, not denied.

It is suggested that we differ in our orientation towards a conflict situation and five basic styles of behaviour can be identified. Most of us will have a preference towards one of the following patterns of behaviour when we are engaged in a conflict situation:

- *Dominance*: a desire to win the conflict situation and overwhelm the other person

- *Collaborative*: this is a problem-solving approach since the individual has a desire to satisfy the wishes of all parties to the conflict by finding an outcome that is acceptable to everyone.
- *Compromise*: the individual is content if he/she gets part of their wants satisfied; this involves giving something to get something, usually by 'splitting the difference'
- *Avoidance*: a low tolerance for conflict tends to force the individual to retreat from the conflict situation
- *Accommodative*: this is also known as 'non-assertion'; it is a 'smoothing' approach whereby the individual tends to focus on the needs, wants and desires of the other person and ignores their own rights.

Understanding your orientation and the possible orientation of others involved in a conflict situation can help you manage the event more effectively. Finding a 'win-win' conflict reduction method should be your aim, unless you have decided that the conflict is, in some way, functional. The use of problem solving to find and address the cause of the conflict is a 'win-win' strategy since each person gets what he/she wants. Thus, conflict is not automatically a negative experience since it creates constructive opportunities for discovering creative solutions. The identification of a superordinate goal, (for example, a group-based incentive) which compels all parties in conflict to cooperate, because alone they cannot achieve the goal, is also a 'win-win' method of conflict reduction.

'Role exchange', that is 'walking a mile in the other person's shoes', can also be a beneficial approach to resolving a conflict situation between two people or among groups and teams. However, both parties or groups must express a desire for change in the status quo.

Managing your anger

Think about the difficult person who is arousing your anger:

- try to diagnose why they are behaving in this way
- is the situation exacerbating the problem?
- what is the trigger to the behaviour?
- are you the cause of their behaviour?
- how did you react in this situation?
- is this a 'one-off' or a pattern of events with this person?

Acknowledge your feelings:

- why do you feel angry?
- are your feelings justified?
- are *you* being aggressive in your anger?
- are you being difficult?
- do you feel in control or overwhelmed?
- are you being realistic about the situation?
- are you jumping to conclusions?

Stay in control:

- remember to keep calm and controlled
- take a few deep breaths; breathe from the diaphragm and force your stomach muscles out, to help you breathe slowly and deeply; briefly pause and hold your breath before you exhale
- controlled breathing will buy you some thinking time and help you to delay your first utterance, thus controlling what you actually say
- use silent 'self-talk' to acknowledge how you are feeling; remember that some people will try to provoke you to anger because they find this situation rewarding. Acknowledging this will help you to stay in control of the situation.

Think about what you will do next:

- ignore the situation or respond?
- if someone insults us, it is important to remember that we do not have to either defend or prove ourselves
- decide what you want to get out of the situation
- do you need more information before you can respond appropriately?

If you are going to respond, say how you are feeling:

- avoid the 'yes, but' approach because it usually results in the other person digging in their heels and defending their own position. An argument will be the most likely outcome of this tactic
- avoid being confrontational: aggression breeds aggression
- use empathetic assertion techniques; this is active listening towards the other person, to show that you have heard what they are saying, respect them, and take them seriously. This is not easy to do because your anger will drive you to speak your mind and ensure that the other person hears your opinion. Using empathy means being able to put yourself in the other person's shoes and understand their feelings, but it will also allow you to talk about your feelings in a direct, positive manner and say clearly what you want to happen. For example, 'when you behave towards me like that it makes me feel ... and it has ... effect on my behaviour. Can we ... discuss/negotiate, etc?
- if the other person is angry it is often best to let them run out of steam before beginning a discussion.

Practise 'self-talk' so you will be trained to deliver the right response and cope when you anger is provoked:

- master and learn phrases to use in maintaining control when you feel you are becoming angry

- use visual imagery to imagine yourself behaving in a controlled way when provoked.

Use assertion skills to avoid becoming aggressive. This involves both verbal and non-verbal aspects of behaviour. The characteristics of these 'difficult' colleagues are described in the chapters above. Use these lists and questionnaires to identify your behaviour and the way you tend to behave when you become angry. Change the way you relate to the other person by being assertive, rather than becoming aggressive or angry. Ultimately it means that you refuse to allow another person to control your behaviour.

Dealing with criticism

Dealing with 'difficult' people at work is likely to require us to both receive and give criticism and many people find this difficult to do effectively. The following guidelines will help to reduce the pressures that we experience when both giving and receiving criticism. The key phrases to remember are: remain calm; stay positive; be objective; use brief, clear statements; be constructive

It helps if we remember that criticism should be directed at the behaviour which we are finding difficult (and is having a negative impact on our own behaviour, performance or well-being) rather than the personality or attitudes of the other person.

If someone makes a personal attack on you, the only productive way of dealing with this is to be assertive. By resorting to aggressive or non-assertive behaviours the situation will become worse and the outcome will be unfavourable. You have the right to ask the other person not to personalize an attack. Other people do have a right to criticize you. However, you also have the right not to be put down, humiliated, or criticized in front of other people.

If you become angry, annoyed or scared, it is likely that you will fail to listen to what is being said during the inter-action and will react inappropriately. Try to relax by taking a few deep breaths. This will also prevent you from speaking too soon and will ensure that you are clear about what is being said about your behaviour or performance. If the criticism is vague or ambiguous, ask the person to be more specific and if necessary to quote actual examples.

Ensure that you are not guilty of faulty thinking when either giving or receiving criticism. Use self-talk to examine potentially damaging thoughts.

Faulty thinking errors include: over-generalizing (from one event to another); exaggeration; minimization; black and white thinking; unrealistic expectations; and irrational/illogical assumptions. Ask yourself, is the criticism fair?

If you are receiving criticism it is helpful if you state the criticism in your own words. Use of reflection, or 'active listening' ensures that both parties are clear about what is being said and shows the other person that you under-stand the criticism. You might want to express your feel-ings and comment on the accuracy, timing or frequency of the criticism. When you are being criticized, you must truthfully ask yourself if it is valid judgement. If you agree that it is a valid observation, you must acknowledge this to the other person and ask for further information so you are able to use the criticism to good effect.

If the criticism is done badly and/or your feelings are hurt, it is appropriate to state this in an assertive way. Begin by using the technique of reflecting back what was said to you before stating your feelings. This ensures the other person realizes that you have understood the criti-cism, rather than assuming that you are going to start an argument or disagree.

When giving criticism, state your specific criticism, encourage the other person to respond to you and then move forward by making and agreeing to suggestions for further action. Try to find something positive to say first, but this must be genuine and specific praise, otherwise do not attempt it! Avoid putting the other person in a defensive position by using assertive 'I' statements, rather than 'you' statements which can be perceived as 'blame'. For example, the wrong way to approach a situation is to say, 'You are absolutely useless; the XYZ report is a complete mess again. Get it right or there will be trouble!'

Compare this to: 'I want to talk to you about the XYZ report. Two of the tables were incorrect and the same mistake was also made last month. Why is this happening? (Wait for a response.) How can this be avoided next month?' (or, 'How can you/ we prevent this happening next month?')

If you want to make a complaint, briefly explain how you feel and why and then stay quiet in order to allow the other person to respond. Resist the urge to relieve your tension by continuing to talk. It is an important part of the technique to let the other person feel some pressure in order for them to be able to take responsibility, cooperate and act on your complaint.

If you face outright hostility you can diffuse the situation by stating how you think the other person is feeling, rather than respond by trying to defend yourself, since this latter strategy is more likely to cause an argument. Say, 'Something has clearly upset you. I am sorry about that.' or 'I am very surprised to hear you say that. Something has clearly upset you.'

Always avoid the temptation to be sarcastic because it shows a lack of respect and implies contempt. Since people are not quite sure what you are getting at, when they do respond, they risk being accused of having no sense of humour or of being too sensitive.

Always summarize what actions have been agreed to ensure that both parties are clear about what they are expected to do in the future. Since the interaction can be laden with emotion, the other person can easily deny or fail to acknowledge the outcome if you do not clarify the anticipated outcome.

The pace of this type of dialogue can often move very fast and develop into an argument if one or the other individual fails to adopt an assertive approach. Try to remember to stay calm, control your breathing and speak slowly and quietly to avoid any escalation of the situation.

Role negotiation

This technique is based on an idea originally described by Roger Harrison in 1972. It is a useful way of overcoming the problems that lead to ineffectiveness caused by behaviour that an individual is unwilling to change, because it would mean a loss of power or influence. Harrison believes that this method works because most people prefer a fair, negotiated settlement to a state of unresolved conflict. Thus, they will be motivated to engage in some action themselves and make concessions in order to achieve this aim.

In role negotiation:

- the change effort is focused solely on the working relationships among the people involved
- the likes and dislikes for one another in the relationship are avoided
- the issues of personal feelings of the people involved are avoided
- an imposed structure is created to allow a controlled negotiation to take place. Each person involved discusses

and agrees in writing to change certain behaviours, in return for changes in behaviour by the other party

- each person asks for changes in the behaviour of the other party which would permit them to do their own job more effectively, in exchange for changing some aspect of their own behaviour, which would serve to improve the effectiveness of the other party involved. Therefore an accurate diagnosis of the problem is necessary
- It is crucial to avoid generalities and be specific. That is, you would ask the other person, to perhaps: 'Stop doing ...', 'Do more of ...', 'Do less of ...'. In turn, these are the types of action that they will ask of you. Ensuring that a diagnosis is carried out as the first step in role negotiation helps to overcome the problems of generalizing comments or resorting to personalized attacks.
- all requests and agreements must be in writing
- each person must give something in order to get something; that is, 'If you do X I will do Y.'
- if one party reneges on their part of the bargain, the whole contract becomes invalid

This technique can be used within a group, to negotiate among team members, or between the team leader or manager and their team. Often the use of an outside facilitator is used for optimum effectiveness. Some progress follow-up is required to determine whether the contracts are being honoured and to assess the effectiveness of the approach.

Managing your own Type A behaviour

If you have identified your style of behaviour as 'Type A' rather than the 'Type B' pattern, the following suggestions might be helpful in minimizing the potentially damaging elements of your behavioural tendencies.

Type A individuals are not good listeners; they tend to speak for others, and even finish their sentences for them. Therefore, try to restrain yourself from being the centre of attention by constantly talking. Force yourself to listen to other people by remembering the axiom, 'We have two ears, but only one mouth – use them in these proportions!' Prepare a small cue card to take into meetings, that says:

MANAGING TYPE A BEHAVIOUR

Listen more ... Don't talk too much

- **Do I really have anything important to say?**
- **Does anyone want to hear it?**
- **Is this the time to say it?**

Remember to thank your colleagues or subordinates when they have performed services for you.

Try to control your obsessionally time-directed life. Type A individuals are bad at estimating the amount of time they need to complete tasks or make journeys. Since you have this tendency to underestimate the passing of time, work out the time you think you need, and then add on extra time – at least ten minutes. This will help to prevent you from driving in a 'white-knuckle' manner from place to place, and going through traffic lights on 'deep amber'. Make sure you always carry something to read, so if you arrive early for an appointment you will not become impatient because you feel you are wasting time. Ultimately your goal should be to try to sit, relax, absorb the environment around you, unwind and mentally prepare yourself for the meeting.

However, this strategy can initially create too much stress for the Type A individual. Gradually build up your toleration for being kept waiting by deliberately exposing yourself to situations where this is likely to happen. Use 'self-talk' to ensure that you do not become impatient or angry; smile, look around and 'take time to smell the roses'. Think about something pleasant that is going to happen soon and make sure that you reward yourself for controlling your time-directed life.

Don't try to do six tasks at once!

Try to remember that the majority of your work does not require immediate action and that a slower, more deliberate pace might result in better quality decisions and judgement. When you feel under pressure, ask yourself, 'Will this matter have any importance five years from now?' and, 'Must I do this right now or do I have enough time to think about the best way to accomplish it?' It is vital to accept that a successful life is always unfinished and so it must be structured around uncompleted tasks and events; only a corpse is completely finished!

Reduce your workaholic tendencies by engaging in social activities outside work. Do not succumb to hard-driving, achievement-oriented, impatient behaviours as part of these interests. If the activity creates feelings of hostility, anger or irritation, do not do it! For example, if you have just thrown your second set of golf clubs into the lake because you do not yet have a 'scratch' game, then golf is not for you. So engage in hobbies, music, art, theatre, and nature etc which encourage you to remain calm, without triggering your natural Type A tendencies. The aim is to establish a realistic balance between professional and personal life activities and achievements.

Avoid setting unrealistic goals and deadlines for yourself and other people.

Cease trying to be an idealist because it is likely to simply end-up in disappointment and hostility towards others.

Do not bottle up emotions or anger because this is extremely damaging. Find ways to 'vent steam'. For example, vigorous physical activity; write that 'angry' letter, but keep it somewhere safe until you calm down and can read it again, before deciding on the best course of action; talk to trusted friends or colleagues about your thoughts, fears and anxieties.

Learn to say 'No' in order to protect your time. Stop trying to prove yourself!

Avoid working for long periods of time without taking a break or 'breathing space' since this is not an effective work strategy. A break helps to take the pressure and tension out of the task and refreshes you ready for action again. Get completely away from the work area and engage in something that is not related to the task. Make sure you take work breaks and a lunch break, preferably in the company of colleagues. Type As often think that time spent in social interchange is 'wasted time', when in fact, they should realize that time spent this way is beneficial.

Monitor the number of times a week you are the first person to arrive and the last person to leave the place of work! Is this really necessary? Resolve to arrive last and leave first at least twice during the week.

Take all your holiday allocation and ensure that your staff follow your example.

Take regular exercise; learn and use some form of relaxation technique.

Do not expect to totally change your behaviour from the 'Type A' to the 'Type B' style. This is an unrealistic and impossible goal. Trying to get a hare to move around just like a tortoise is evolutional suicide; just ask the fox! Recognize and accept your limitations, but gradually begin to take more control of your drive to be Type A.

Managing the 'difficult' behaviour of your Type A boss or colleague

Attempt to raise awareness in the Type A individual to the dangers and drawbacks of their style of behaviour. Explain that their behaviour can be counter-productive for them and for those around them. If you are both Type A, agree to help each other change the damaging aspects of your behaviour (especially, hostility!). Remember, Type A behaviour is not all bad and can lead to career success and satisfaction.

Avoid becoming angry and challenging the Type A individual; this will only exacerbate their behaviour and foster aggressive and hostile feelings.

Type As have a strong need to be in control and become highly distressed when they perceive a loss of personal control over events around them. Use of the role negotiation technique already described might help you to cope with this Type A tendency.

If you are the boss of Type A employees (and are probably a Type A yourself) try to avoid a 'working long hours' culture by setting an example and making it plain that the organization will not reward individuals for 'losing themselves in their work'. Consistently working at weekends and taking work home every night is not an acceptable or efficient long-term work strategy. While the individual continues to receive reward in the form of promotion and recognition, this workaholic lifestyle will be perpetuated. Breaking the pattern of this mode of working will not be easy because the organization is gaining certain and immediate benefits, whereas the drawbacks (or punishment) in the form of premature death, forced early retirement, sickness absence, additional recruitment and training costs, poor company image, and stress litigation claims are uncertain and delayed.

Encourage the Type A individual to take work breaks and join you for lunch.

Talk openly about your feelings, concerns and fears in the hope that the Type A individual will reciprocate. This will help to create and develop a climate of trust and openness, which contributes to a more supportive work environment.

Use the skills of assertion to prevent the Type A colleague or boss from setting unrealistic time deadlines and goals for you. They have a tendency to underestimate how long a task will take and so you must be assertive with them, in order to prevent time-pressure demands. Use the broken record technique to refuse a request, to get the Type A individual or boss to listen to you or your ideas, or to get a message across. It means persistence. You simply repeat your message in a calm, thoughtful way until it gets through; it is not nagging or whining! To do this successfully you need to use the same words over and over again in different sentences.

For example, 'I cannot have the export report ready in five days' time. I already have X to do which is urgent, and this will take me three days, so I cannot have the report ready in five days' time. I will start working on it as soon as X is finished, but I cannot have the export report ready in five days' time.'

When working with a Type A colleague include some time for 'the unexpected' in a work schedule because the Type A individual is unlikely to do this!

Dealing with the abrasive personality

The strategy to use in dealing with an abrasive personality will, of course, depend on whether the individual is a colleague or boss. Some of the strategies already described above will be useful (for example, role negotiation, and handling criticism), but in addition, certain specific tactics can be used.

Try to identify ways in which you change difficult aspects of behaviour by using the technique of non-reward. For example, discourage the abrasive individual from dominating the discussion by eliciting the help of the chairperson, who can ensure that people only speak through 'the chair'. By only responding to requests to speak if the individual is not dominating, arguing or attacking, the undesirable behaviour can be modified. Ensuring that the person does not receive a 'reward' for their behaviour is a powerful motivation to change.

Use of brain-storming is a technique that will also help to prevent the abrasive personality from dominating a meeting. It entails generating ideas and solutions to a problem by suspending all criticism and evaluation until all the possible options have been identified. Everyone present is invited, in turn, to offer ideas, which are written on a flip chart, without prejudice or judgement, before the discussion and debate session is opened.

Recognize that the abrasive personality is trying to do the best they can and should be given respect. This will enable you to open a discussion which is not confrontational and damaging to self-image.

Try not to be critical and stick to the facts about specific behaviours rather than discussing generalities about personality or emotions.

Ask the individual to reflect on how he/she thinks that

the other person is feeling or acting in response to the abrasive outburst.

Ask what goal he/she expects to achieve in the interaction

Explain how you feel in response to their abrasive style of behaviour. That is, talk about your irritation and anger and why you perceive this type of behaviour to be self-defeating.

Use the appraisal situation to provide feedback about 'difficult' behaviour. Agree and set goals for a change in behaviour.

Levinson suggests that you are likely to learn lots by tolerating an abrasive boss for a limited time because they often have very high standards, and so have much to teach. However, the abrasive boss is unlikely to tolerate you once you start to 'chafe under their rigid control' and begin to assert yourself. This might be the time to consider a change of boss, since it is unlikely that you will be able change your abrasive boss when powerful superiors have not been successful, or have decided that he/she is more useful to the organization by behaving in this manner.

If *you* are the abrasive personality it is important that you monitor your interactions with other people to ensure that your style of behaviour is not, in the long-term, costly to yourself and the people around you. Elicit the help of a close colleague ('a buddy'), who is willing to give you honest and direct feedback. However, you must be prepared to handle any criticism assertively, without becoming abrasive or angry, and ask for help. This is a sign of strength, not weakness.

Dealing with the aggressive personality

It is important that you diffuse aggression and avoid resorting to aggression and anger in yourself when confronted by aggression. Coping with aggression is demanding and it is often easier, in the short-term, to retaliate with either an aggressive or non-assertive response. However, it is unlikely that you will be happy about the outcomes in the long-term. So, it is worthwhile to persevere and try to actively manage the aggressive, difficult person. Not all situations can follow a rigid step-by-step approach but the following guidelines can help.

- Gain control of your thoughts and feelings by breathing correctly. This buys you some time to slow down the fast pace of an aggressive interaction.
- Pause and then gain information by asking questions to ensure that you understand the circumstances and situation. Encourage the aggressor to talk about the feelings that are causing their aggressive behaviour.
- Check your own inner dialogue for faulty thinking: Are you harbouring unrealistic or irrational beliefs?
- Use empathetic listening to show the other person that you understand what they are saying, that you respect them and take them seriously.
- Clarifying any discrepancies that exist. Aggressive behaviour often arises from misunderstandings.
- Explain how you are feeling and the impact of their behaviour on your actions.
- Discuss alternative behaviour or actions.
- If aggression is maintained, cut off the interaction by leaving the situation.
- Try to find or see points in the other person's argument with which you can agree.
- Use the broken record technique to refuse a request; get someone to listen to you or your ideas; to get a message across (see page 53).
- Remember the power of silence; do not be afraid to maintain silence to gain control in an aggressive interaction.
- Practise saying, 'No'.

- Use the fogging technique to diffuse the aggressive interaction. This approach allows you to recognize what is happening without agreeing with it so that you do not become either defensive or aggressive. You are not required to back down or agree with the attack. For example, if a colleague says, 'You handled that deal ineffectively and acted weakly by letting them get away with it', you say, 'Yes, I can see that you feel I acted in a weak manner.'

7

ACTION PLANNING

The first step in action planning is to undertake an accurate diagnosis of the problem. Self-assessment and analysis of the perceived problem can be carried out by using the questionnaires in this book; by keeping a daily log of behaviour, interactions and critical events; or by eliciting feedback from others. Actively encouraging constructive feedback about your own behaviour towards other people in the workplace can be a powerful motivation to change. Indeed, if we can adopt this strategy with our colleagues, it is likely that they will reciprocate and thereby provide us with an opportunity to provide them with feedback about aspects of their behaviour which we find difficult *and* which has some negative impact on our own performance, well-being or quality of work life. Only when we have this information can we begin our action planning.

Step One: Identify your goals and objectives

What do you want to achieve?
Write a goal statement which includes your specific

objectives. The rules of goal writing suggest that goals must be 'SMART'. This means they are:

Specific
Measurable
Achievable
Realistic
Time-banded

Step Two: Prioritize your goals and objectives

Rank your goals in terms of

A – must do
B – would like to do
C – can wait

and

1 – high threat
2 – medium threat
3 – low threat

This will help you to decide what to do first. Do not assume that you should tackle an 'A1' goal immediately. This is the trap that usually befalls the Type A individual! You will gain more benefit by initially tackling a lower priority goal in order to learn and practise your new skills (eg assertiveness). When you have become skilled and more confident, tackle a high-priority and high-threat goal with a greater chance of success.

Step Three: Identify the strategies and the approach to be used

Make a list of the options available and rate them in terms of their attractiveness to you (eg ease, comfort, potential threat to self-esteem); your perceptions about the outcomes, that is the chance of success or failure. For example, in dealing with difficult people, we can decide to:

- do nothing
- compromise
- learn to live with the situation
- procrastinate or play for time
- confront the person
- get someone else to handle the situation for you
- learn and use certain skills such as:
  1. assertion
  2. using an appropriate style of leadership
  3. conflict management
  4. anger management
  5. the management of meetings
  6. role negotiation.

Step Four: Schedule your activities

Draw up a timetable for your activities or actions. This should be used as your implementation plan and must specifically state how you intend to achieve your aims and goals.

Step Five: Share and discuss your plan with another person or group

You are more likely to stay committed to a plan of action if you share your ideas and goals with other people. This declaration will help you to stick to your objective. Ideally, use another person as a 'buddy' and ask them to check on your progress at regular intervals. If you reciprocate an act as a 'buddy' for the other person you will develop a bond which will strengthen goal commitment and the likelihood of success.

Step Six: Monitor progress

Keep a log in which you write about your progress. This can be a daily or weekly log; or one in which you just monitor critical events. Typically, you could write about:

- the situation
- what you did (the behaviour)
- who else was involved in the interaction
- what the other person(s) did (their behaviour)
- what should you have done?
- on reflection – what were your thoughts and feelings during and after the event?
- what were the satisfactory aspects of your performance or behaviour?
- what aspects of your performance (behaviour) need to be improved?

Step Seven: Evaluate progress

At regular intervals measure your success by critically analysing your progress and, if necessary, reconsider the strategy. This will be easier to do if you have kept a written log. Also, the use of your 'buddy' will help you to be objective in this exercise.

Step Eight: Reward success

It is often difficult to work towards a distant goal because the reward is too remote. Overcome this problem by setting interim targets which will progressively move towards goal achievement. Make sure that you reward yourself for success at each target stage and on achievement of your goal.

A FINAL WORD

Life might be more pleasant if you can just learn to accept difficult people for what they are rather than devoting much time and energy into trying to change them, or yourself! Ultimately, the situation might exist because of the way in which you react and you end up with a problem, rather than them. In order to be able to be more tolerant of difficult people we need to:

- accept other people for what they are
- remember that no one is perfect, least of all *ourselves*
- try to recognize and focus on the positive qualities of the other person
- build and maintain a high level of self-esteem. If you 'like' yourself and feel good about the way you look, think and feel, it is less likely that the 'difficult' person is going to get under your skin and allow you to become irritated and angry
- stay in control and do not let the other person affect your behaviour and life. We will only experience our encounter with the 'difficult person' as stressful when we perceive a

lack of control or a sense of helplessness over the situation and interaction
- accept that if we adopt a rigid style of behaviour and remain inflexible, we will create barriers to our acceptance of the 'other person' for what they are
- remember, personal mastery of a difficult situation, which avoids damage to our self-esteem, is highly rewarding and satisfying. It makes you feel 'good' and helps to build the 'virtuous circle' of self-worth, happiness and well-being, rather than ending up in a vicious downward spiral of misery and despair, because we have reacted adversely to someone at work who has behaved in a 'difficult' way.

And keep in mind,

WE ALL HAVE THE CAPACITY TO BE 'DIFFICULT'

Ultimately, we should keep in mind that humour is a very effective way of dealing with a difficult person or situation. So remember, as Ella Wilcox says,

Laugh and the world laughs with you ... weep and you weep alone.

(from 'Solitude')

REFERENCES

Bortner, RW, (1969) 'A short rating scale as a potential measure of pattern A behaviour' *Journal of Chronic Diseases,* 22, 87–91.

Friedman, MD and Rosenman, RH (1974) *Type A Behaviour and Your Heart,* Knopf; New York

Harrison, R (1972) 'When power conflicts trigger team spirit' *European Business,* Spring, pp 27–65.

Heron, J (1977) *Catharsis in Human Development,* Human Potential Research Project, University of Guildford; Surrey.

Levinson, H (1978) 'The abrasive personality' *Harvard Business Review,* May–June pp 86–94.

Wolf, SG (1960), in Lewis H, Griswold H, and Underwood H (eds) *Stress and Heart Disease. Modern Concepts of Cardiovascular Disease.* American Heart Association; New York. **29**, pp 559–603.

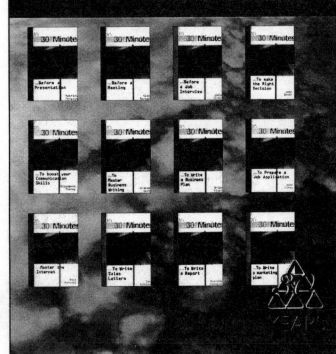